Meet my neighbor, the artist

Marc Crabtree

Author and Photographer

⚘ Crabtree Publishing Company

www.crabtreebooks.com

🌴 Crabtree Publishing Company

Meet my neighbor, the artist

For David and Sonya, with thanks

Author and photographer
Marc Crabtree

Editor
Reagan Miller

Design
Samantha Crabtree

Production coordinator
Margaret Amy Salter

Glossary
Crystal Sikkens

Photographs
All photographs by Marc Crabtree except:
Shutterstock: page 3

Library and Archives Canada Cataloguing in Publication

Crabtree, Marc
    Meet my neighbor, the artist / author and photographer, Marc
Crabtree.

(Meet my neighbor)
ISBN 978-0-7787-4569-3 (bound).--ISBN 978-0-7787-4579-2 (pbk.)

    1. Scott, David--Juvenile literature. 2. Painting--Juvenile literature.
3. Painters--Biography--Juvenile literature. I. Title. II. Series: Crabtree,
Marc . Meet my neighbor.

ND1146.C73 2009   j750   C2009-900420-8

Library of Congress Cataloging-in-Publication Data

Crabtree, Marc.
  Meet my neighbor, the artist / author and photographer, Marc
Crabtree.
      p. cm. -- (Meet my neighbor)
  ISBN 978-0-7787-4579-2 (pbk. : alk. paper) -- ISBN 978-0-7787-4569-3
(reinforced library binding : alk. paper)
  1. Painting--Juvenile literature. 2. Painters--Juvenile literature.
I. Title.
  ND1146.C7 2009
  750--dc22
                                          2009001567

Crabtree Publishing Company

www.crabtreebooks.com   1-800-387-7650

Published in Canada
Crabtree Publishing
616 Welland Ave.
St. Catharines, Ontario
L2M 5V6

Published in the United States
Crabtree Publishing
PMB16A
350 Fifth Ave., Suite 3308
New York, NY 10118

Published in the United Kingdom
Crabtree Publishing
White Cross Mills
High Town, Lancaster
LA1 4XS

Published in Australia
Crabtree Publishing
386 Mt. Alexander Rd.
Ascot Vale (Melbourne)
VIC 3032

Meet my Neighbor

Contents

Meet my neighbor, David Scott, the artist. David and his wife Sonya are playing with their son Del in their backyard.

David shows his son how he paints. The owner of the house in the **painting** asked David to paint a picture of it.

David mixes his paints on a **palette**. The palette is a large piece of glass.

Artists mix **colors** to make new colors.

10

Yellow and blue make green. Red and yellow make orange.

11

David also paints animal pictures. This picture shows two ducks. They are sleeping with their heads tucked under their wings to keep warm.

This is David's painting of a starling on a statue.

This is David's painting of a bald eagle.

David draws a picture of a pumpkin. He uses a **magnifying glass** to see exactly what he is doing.

David uses a sharp **pencil** to draw the pumpkin.

David makes a **drawing** of a beautiful seashell from the ocean.

David's **picture framer** displays David's drawings of birds and homes.

20

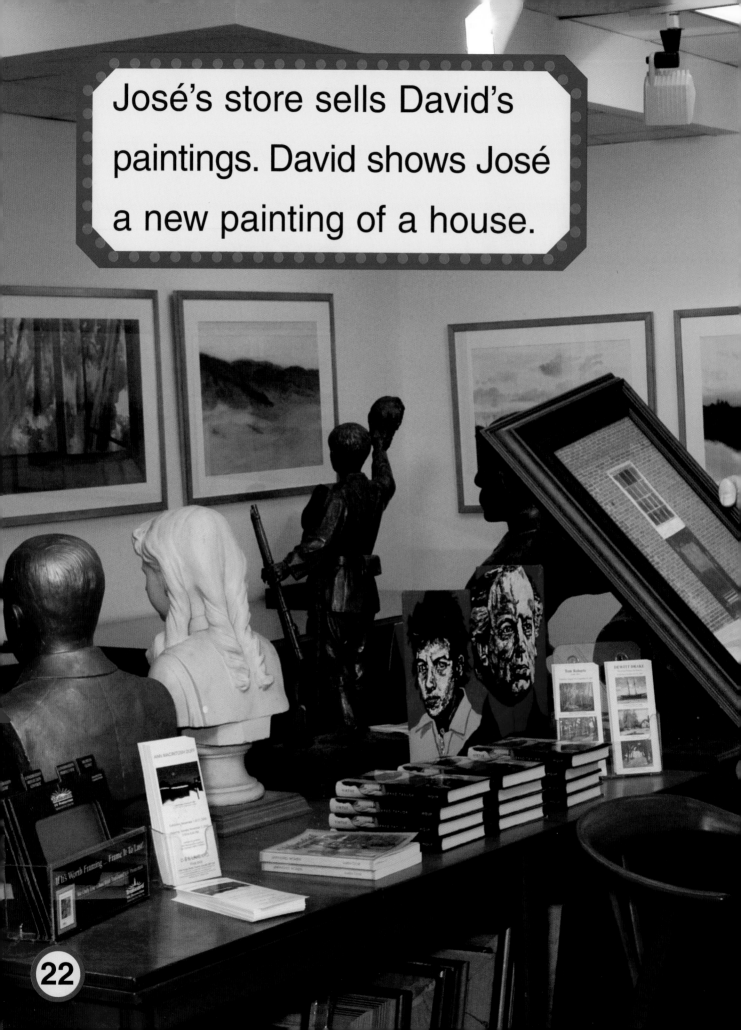

José's store sells David's paintings. David shows José a new painting of a house.

23

Glossary

colors

drawing

magnifying glass

painting

frame

palette

pencil

picture frame

Printed in the U.S.A. - CG